Millionaire

Living It

Shelley Zegers
MP Publishing

Copyright

© 2018 by Shelley Zegers

All rights reserved. This book or any portion thereof may not be reproduced or used in any manner whatsoever without the express written permission of the publisher except for the use of brief quotations in a book review.

Table of Content

ACKNOWLEDGEMENTS 5

INTRODUCTION 8

ONE 10

WHY WOULD YOU WANT TO BE A MILLIONAIRE? 10

TWO 14

HOW WILL YOU BECOME A MILLIONARE? 14
1. RECOGNIZE WHAT YOU DO BEST. 15
2. DON'T MAKE BEING A MILLIONAIRE YOUR PURPOSE. 17
3. MONEY DOES NOT DEFINE YOU AS A PERSON. 18
4. TAKE IT EASY ON YOURSELF 19
5. MAKE MISTAKES 21
6. BE BRAVE ENOUGH TO BE BROKE 22
7. BELIEVE 23

THREE 25

WILL YOU BE A SUCCESSFUL MILLIONAIRE? 25

FOUR 29

WOULD YOU RATHER LIVE A SIMPLE LIFE? 29

WHAT SCARES PEOPLE FROM LIVING A SIMPLE LIFE? 29

WHY WOULD I WANT A SIMPLE LIFE? 31

FIVE 34

ARE YOU DESIGNED TO LIVE FOR A WEALTHY LIFESTYLE? 34

CONCLUSION 40

ABOUT THE AUTHOR 42

Acknowledgements

I would like to send all my thanks to the team who continues to give me endless opportunities to share my thoughts, and extend my heartfelt messages to the world. If not for you, I would not have had the chance to make a great beginning. I will continue to pour my knowledge and love to doing what I do best—and it is writing. This book had been a challenge for me to write, as if it was not meant for me. But you believed that I have something incredibly relevant to share and you never stopped encouraging me to work on it, and so, here it is now, I could not have been any prouder than this!

Thanks to the whole society, as well. This book is absolutely inspired with what I would have wanted to tell my fellowmen—each one of you walking down the many streets of this world. I know we all want to make it big somewhere, and I know that we are all different no matter how common the needs are of all the others. I will do my best to make sure that this book helps you find your inner peace and your inner piece in this universe.

To my family, of course, who is always part of all of every success that I have in my life. People say they admire my passion, and how big of a fan I am with love. Whatever I am right now is something that was molded by the way that I was brought up in this world. I live a simple life, and I can say that I am one of the most grateful persons in the world—why? Because I have you. Because I am richer than that kind of "rich" that everybody talks about. Our family may not be perfect, but we perfectly know that we are strong together. You will always be the biggest part of my whole being, and no one will ever be able to take that away.

To You, my Lord Father God: You always guide me in a way that no one could ever explain. There is no science that could tell for sure just how powerful Your love is for us and I am just very blessed to be able to acknowledge that. I thank You as You guide me while I write every single word that I will spread for the world to see. I am complete because You are in me: You are in my soul, my heart, You are in my whole entire being. I believe that I am one spec of light that came from Your holiness, so it is my duty to make sure that I promote selflessness and show what love means for me.

Introduction

Who wants to be a Millionaire? Who wants to be rich? Who wants power? Who wants to be known as one of the most relevant people in the world? If you do want to be any one of those, is it a bad thing? Is it a sin to want to be big?

One thing that I want to let everyone know--at least in my own opinion--is that, it is not bad to want something for yourself. You as an individual deserve every single best thing that you could possibly have in mind; and you know what 'best' means when it comes to your own self by default whether you are aware of it or not. You know in your heart what you want. You will recognize when it is for you if it is for you. It is your duty to fight for it, and to have it.

When you should ever become a millionaire, what would you do? Will your life be better? This book will open up opportunities for understanding what wealth really means, and hopefully allow you to manage your path towards it. Here are the things that we will talk about:

1. Why would you want to become a millionaire?
2. How will you become a millionaire?
3. Will you be a successful millionaire?
4. Would you rather have a simple life?
5. Are you designed to live for a wealthy lifestyle?

And then after you are done with this book, I hope you would take away with you some facts about yourself, and about this broad meaning of being a millionaire.

ONE

Why would you want to be a Millionaire?

Try to answer the question. Do not hesitate, because this is just a reflection. No one will or can judge you, and it would be up to you if you wish to tell the world what your answer is. But whatever your answer is going to be, I hope that it would lead to also being able to react to the other four questions that are remaining for you to address as you read along.

Why would you want to be a Millionare? This question could either seem too vague, too complex, too obvious, and it could also be too rude. I mean, why would you have to be asked such question, right? But, really, if the Universe were to make someone a millionaire based on their purpose, do you think your answer would convince it enough to give you the opportunity that you are longing for? I am not saying that you should want to be rich so that people could depend on you. In fact, we are talking about you.

Most of the people, especially those like me who come from a very low key kind of status in life, would pretty much want to be rich! Do I want to be rich? Oh yes! But we all need to understand that being rich is not just all that. Imagine the people who won the lottery, for an instance. Just think about how many lottery tickets they may have paid for, just for that one odd shot that maybe they might be the lucky one to hit the jackpot! And then there is the winning! Boom! Instantly, John Bush is a millionaire (I made that name up). What is next for him, then? Does this make him popular? Does this make his life easier because he could spend his money to pay people to work for him and do things for him? Or will it make things more complicated because money could put someone's life in danger?

I recall being in a room filled with people, and the facilitator asked random individuals about what they would do should they suddenly earn themselves millions. One person said she would quit her job and travel the world; another one said he would buy more cars; another one said she would start her own business; another one would fulfill each and every activity she listed in her bucket list; and then another one said he would donate it to charity. Which ones resonated to you most? Did you hate one of those ideas and think that one person is better than the other? Well, if we will just look at it at the surface, maybe. But if you would let each of them explain why and where those answer would actually lead to in the long run, it might change your mind.

What if the girl who said she would quit her job and travel the world becomes successful in a way that she travels the world and learn many different cultures that would eventually enrich her way of thinking about life, and then maybe brings home barely a good amount of money but an incredible amount of wisdom that she would share with the people? And then that guy who said he would give the money away to charity just does that and then stops from there, only because she does not really care what happens with the money or where it goes, that he also cares less about the community where it would be given away to?

Unless you really give something or someone a chance, you will never know, right? How will you make it right? As human beings, we ought to realize that we play a huge and essential role in this whole Universe. It is definitely okay to want something for yourself. Actually, know what you want, and what makes you happy. Know your inner being. Connect deeply into your soul and it would not be so hard anymore to decide why you would want to be rich. Because when you do, it will all lead to something great, and something really special.

TWO

How will you become a millionare?

Believe it or not, the easiest question to answer here is the 'How will you become a millionaire?'. Simple. Do your best at what you do. Dedicate time to be successful, and do not overspend your money. Manage your finances as you continue to earn them. Work really hard!

Stop listening to people that are trying to put you down. That crab mentality is just not going to be popular if no one allows himself to be a victim. The more you let yourself get affected by those rude words from others that are not happy to see you succeed in life, the more they tend to win over you.

Here are my lucky seven great ways to be a millionaire:

1. Recognize what you do best.

Do you write well? Are you a good singer? Is Math your forte? Do you have a very creative mind? Do you play instruments? I mean I could go on and on and mention a lot of different talents. We are all born with something special in us. All it takes is for us to recognize them. Know yourself. Open up and let your inner person get out of the shell and play a big part of your entirety. You can go places if you do share that talent to the world. People will demand to see what you got to offer, and witness your incredible skills, so, go ahead and entertain!

Once you have acknowledged what you are good at and walk on to this life doing what you do best,

Will pretty much enjoy being that person that you are. You will be known for that skill by many people. You will eventually be in demand because the society would build respect out of what you contribute to the public, and then you will continue to grow through that passion, as you strive to perfect the best thing that you do in life.

Al Heist is one of my childhood friends. He is a really talented violinist, who grew up with his grandmother. When we were younger, myself, with three other friends would hang out at Al's house after school. He owns a drum set other than a violin and I would bring my guitar, our other friend would bring a bass guitar and we would just keep playing songs for hours until we notice just how much we have perfected each song. As we grew older, some of the kids from school would make fun of Al because he had never entered a relationship in high school because he was too dedicated with his music. He was rumored to being gay, and people would talk about him behind his back saying that he was just one spoiled rich kid hiding in his house all the time because his grandmother was a witch who did not like letting him socialize with other kids.

Myself, together with one other girl friend ended up just being the ones who would hang out with Al until we finished high school. I had to move out of the state because I got admitted to University in San Diego so I had to live with my cousin. Al and I were able to manage to stay in touch somehow, and whenever I would go home during semestral breaks I was still able to jam with him with two of his new found friends. When we finished college, we got too busy. I was busy with my job, and he was busy still paying the violin.

I heard that he had started playing in cocktails at some hotels in our local town. And then one day I found out that he had already opened his own studio at the town as his own business, where he started to teach music while also accepting gigs for formal gatherings, especially on weddings.

2. Don't make being a millionaire your purpose.

Once you are finally out there as the person that you love, you should nurture that love on what you are. A lot of people are normally just passionate at the beginning because they want to achieve fame that will earn them money in return, because they want to be a millionaire. Most of those that achieve wealth end up not really being able to handle the lifestyle. They lose their focus and lose their grip. Their life begin to revolve around the money that they both make and fail to make, that when they lose the spotlight they end up getting depressed and eventually give up in life.

When you go out in the world to share your special gift from the heavens above, just go and keep on doing what you love. Enjoy it. As you enjoy it, you will learn that you also enjoy making others happy by doing the simplest, easiest things that you know. Is that not a great thing to imagine? I mean, if you are good at art and you paint portraits effortlessly that people appreciate in a way that you never expected, would it not be great to see their happy faces looking at your masterpiece? If we take our focus out of money, making people happy would eventually be something that we would get addicted on. As we work harder to strive to see smile on these people's faces, we would eventually end up continue doing our best at what we do best and before we know it, we already have a rich heart, a rich life, and a rich pocket—with the latter not even being as important as the first two.

3. Money does not define you as a person.

Admit it. People worship money. Does it not sound so bad that we do? Well, it is never too late to change that mind set. If we begin to focus on the quality of life that we have with money not being a factor of it, eventually we will end up earning more and more money and one day just realize we have already saved so much, just because we did not touch the money that much because we only spend for important things. Keeping away from the kind of lifestyle that other people promote in many generations and just living your life without any insecurity, without having to prove ourselves to the world will actually give that every penny not much of a value. What you do in your life matters most. Living a simple but satisfactory, harmless lifestyle is much more important than being able to spend thousands of dollars for a piece of purse or a pair of shoes.

When you are finally able to establish within yourself that you want to earn money but money will never measure your worth, you will always be able to make sure that you would keep a grip of your own life. There was never a price tag attached to your head. Everything that you are, and everything that you do is YOU. Go take the credit for it!

4. Take it easy on yourself.

It is absolutely okay to want to be at your best. But you have to understand that you are only human. The tendency of being a very perfectionist person is that we forget that we are not robots. We are not some characters in the movies who do not seem to feel tired at anything while being spontaneous with their responsibilities.

There are times when we may not seem to do things right. Our head is just not working around what we should be doing. One thing we need to acknowledge is, IT IS OK. Take a deep breath. Take a break. Get up of your seat and walk away from that task for a minute and let your mind roam freely to what is around you. Have a conversation with someone: your friends; your family. Let yourself get right back to the earth and allow the Universe to remind you why you are doing what you are doing in the first place. The things that inspire you are the thoughts that recharge your soul back and prepare you to move forward again even strongly and cleverly.

Live one day at a time, and you can succeed on your plans one try at a time as well. Dare not to look at how fast others move towards their dreams if you are the type of person that is easily influenced. Because when you see them reaching their goals more easily than you do, it would more likely tend to destroy your own focus to where you are going. Who said you are targeting the same goal as they do, anyway? Who told you the roads that work for them would work for you, too? You should understand that these people may be using a different strategy—imagine that like the type of vehicle you are driving, where you could be behind the wheel of a mini van and the person right next to you drives a monster truck. You both have different controls. You both have different wheels. So what is the rush?

The more you put pressure to yourself, the easier you would end up making mistakes. You will panic. You will cram. Take your time. Who is in a hurry, anyway?

5. Make Mistakes

I am not saying that you should purposely make mistakes. I am also not giving you an excuse to mess up. I am only saying that it is alright to take risks, and know that it could be possible that you might at times make the wrong decisions. Of course, it is important to be careful. Before you pick your choice, you need to be confident with your decisions. But when you happen to screw up the plan, go be the first one to tap yourself and say, 'It's okay. You did what you think is right, and what you think is best'. Remember: your own words of wisdom to yourself are still more assuring than that of other people. Unless you are able to convince yourself of something, no matter what they say and no matter what they do to uplift your spirit will do nothing.

6. Be brave enough to be broke

I know we are talking about making you a millionaire. But admit it or not, this is an essential part of setting your head to getting there. Why do you have to think about being broke? Nope, I did not say you should think of yourself being broke. All you need to do is understand that this could be a possibility sometimes. There are times when you might need to deal with some really heavy challenges of being broke. It is not going to be Christmas the whole year, just like they say.

Be strong enough and brave enough to face the possibility that you might make a hard fall. This is what will make you fearless to getting up much higher up there and make the most out of the opportunities that you get. When you know how to be poor, you will know how to climb the ladder. A person who knows how it is like to be beaten up and how it feels like to be defeated also knows the best ways to get around it. They know a lot of different strategies to survive.

7. Believe

Say, "I can make millions!" Say it again. Okay, now, even louder! Are you inside the bus? Are you I your room? Are you out at the front door? I of course could not hear you, but, if this is really what you want, you should not be ashamed to go say it and be proud to announce this to the world.

I want you to believe on your dreams. If you are dreaming to become a millionaire, go ahead and declare it to the entire Universe. Let the heavens hear what you plan to make out of your life Hopefully you have really good intentions on your wanting to become a millionaire, but it is always going to be up to you.

When you are so sure that you can do something, this is what will continue to drive you to get up in the morning and be the person that you are striving to become. You just bragged about it to the world, right? Then, let the world see how much you want it. Let the world see how much you can do to make it happen. One big secret—this Universe has its own wonderful way of aiding people out when we let it see what we are waking up for!

I guess what I am trying to say here, is, the more we just live our lives naturally without having to try to satisfy the society's destructive standards, it would be much easier to make money. Stop counting. Stop and breathe and just breathe. Just live.

THREE

Will you be a successful millionaire?

Once you have achieved the amount of money that you wished for so long to earn, will you be able to handle it? Do you have the ability to be a successful millionaire? Remember: the question here is whether or not you can be a successful wealthy person or not because we have already established how you could earn money. The real question is whether you can handle a millionaire's life or not.

Just when you thought it would be easy, it may not be. See how I did not completely put the idea of being wealthy in a negative note? This is because we all have a choice whether our lives will be miserable being a millionaire or not. There are people who are able to live a happy life despite the fact that they got plenty of money to manage, while there are people as well you end up unhappy as a rich person.

Would you like to be a happy and successful millionaire? Well, then, do not save that money in your head. When we always keep in mind just how rich we are, we will always have the tendency of believing that we are bigger than everybody else. Just because you are able to buy a sports car so easily in cash unlike your gardener who has to pay for his mini car in installments with the bank, does not make you a much relevant person that he is. Money does not define your place in this world. The moment that this kind of mentality manifests in your head, you will be out. You will definitely be out of the real world, hence you will fail to enjoy life. Because you will only see people that has the same lifestyle as yours. You will think that the average people are less worthy of attention than you are. Even though you make more and more money as the time goes on, getting detached from life is what will make you lose more before your very eyes.

I know a lot of people who would tend to pay for someone to follow them around to run them errands. I guess that is okay especially if you are a really busy person and your job requires so much urgency and you have a target to meet. It is still you working, while getting enough assistance from others that could make you more efficient with what you do.

But if you are just someone who likes to give command on others and enslave them because you are too lazy to put on even your simplest pajamas at night, pour your own milk, pour your own water, slice your own cake, shampoo your own hair, or even open your own car door so you would rather pay someone else to those things for you since you have a handful of money anyway, that is just one big example of a dead person walking around believing he or she is still alive. Do you get the idea? Paying thousands of money just to have someone do almost all of the things for you every day is like not living your life, at all, unless you got a disease that keeps you from really being able to do it.

In my opinion, a successful millionaire is someone who is still able to enjoy life. It is someone who is able to walk around this earth as a human being. It is someone who is not consumed by his wealth; instead, he is the one in control because his money does not own him, he owns it.

People like this are able to wear a genuine smile on their faces each time. All of these people are not easily made insecure by anything or by anyone. They are established, and they are happy. They know what they want, so they are able to do what they really wish to do without any inhibitions.

FOUR

Would you rather live a simple life?

When we talk about simple life, it means living in a way that we are satisfied with the basics. It is not necessarily having to live in poverty, or isolation. A simple life is being able to keep up with only the things that you need. A car, maybe? A house, enough food on the table, a happy family, a good job. Problems and conflicts in life are inevitable, so, do not expect a completely perfect kind of world.

This kind of status in this world has its two faces, though. Like what most people want to know, let us look at its pros and cons.

What scares people from living a simple life?

#1 Money problems!

A simple life can also mean having money problems. Of course, you would have to pay for your bills. But how about those expenses that are already out of your budget?

Everyone gets to experience money issues. It is not a bad thing. We just need to keep a straight mind that understands that it is part of life. The more that we panic, the more that we end up losing the best ideas to deal with problems—may it be monetary or not. So take it easy. There are plenty of resources around you. No matter what happens, you will survive, so do not be afraid to face the challenges.

When things get too much for us, we can borrow money. Is that a bad thing? These days, maybe it has already become quite an embarrassment for some people when they have to borrow money. But let me tell you this—it is only embarrassing to those that are responsible with paying that borrowed money back. I mean, if you are not a good paying person but you still like borrowing money, does that not draw a clear picture that you indeed do not give much of a damn whether you pay it back or not? So, yes—you can borrow money. As long as you are paying it back and you are responsible enough with whatever was loaned to you, you should not feel so bad about it. You just have to make sure that you only borrow what you can pay back.

If you do not like to borrow money, you can also sell some stuff from your house that you do not need anymore. Holding on too much on things will really keep us from moving on to this life and make progress. Sometimes, we actually have those possessions so they could help us someday when we need it—like when we need to sell something out of unforeseen circumstances.

Why would I want a simple life?

Basically, it is really just money matters that keep people from settling in a simple life. But this kind of lifestyle has its own really special perks for us.

Will it not be nice just to be able to sit at the front porch watching some of your neighbors walking their dog early in the morning? Would you not love the idea of being able to say hi to the familiar faces you see at the grocery store, and maybe have a little chat about how their days had been? Driving around town and just enjoy the wonderful clean breeze of fresh air in the late afternoon sounds like fun, too.

Imagine what I just pictured. I would not believe you if you would tell me it did not draw a smile in your head. Some sort of a peace of mind would be such a great thing to treasure all the time.

Many of the Hollywood celebrities that we know have chosen to live this plain and quiet lifestyle even though they got all the money in the world to be treated like kings and queens.

Take Keanu Reeves for example. He is one of the most popular actors in the world, selling out movies here and there. His fame began when he starred in movies like in the Bill and Ted franchise, Speed (my favorite), John Wick franchise, The Devil's Advocate, and especially the series The Matrix. He has so many more incredibly big movies but he has stayed humble and simple all these years despite the fame. He had been through a lot, but one of the highlights of his life that proves he is not owned by his riches is the fact that he makes films regardless of how much he gets offered on for as long as he believes in the story and sees himself really being part of it. He also has put up a cancer charity requesting not to tie his name up to it. He said, "Money is the last thing I think about." He had just recently purchased his own house, but had been very comfortable all these years to commute, hang out in public like everybody else, and ride his motor bike around. He may not have necessarily said it, but, it is very obvious that Keanu was not, and has never been consumed by his fame. I mean, paparazzis will only chase you if you run, right? For Keanu, things can be simple and you do not have to try too hard to be recognized as a celebrity. It just goes to show that we all have a choice of how we will make people treat us.

Life is not perfect only because we picture the idea of it being perfect based on what other people make of it. And this generation has just been pinning that anything that is perfect is anything that is impossible. Have your own self understanding of what you really see and what you really feel. It is not on them to decide whether you are happy or not, because you are the one who will determine what it is exactly that you feel. Money will not be able to buy that.

FIVE

Are you designed to live for a wealthy lifestyle?

I guess I have pretty much sold out to you the simple kind of living, huh? Here is the twist. You can be both simple but wealthy at the same time. All it takes is being able to strike a balance between the two.

I have talked about what is scaring people from living a simple life, right? Now, what scares some of us—ironically—of being a rich person?

Many rich people end up getting taken advantage on. They get to be surrounded by a huge crowd, with not a single one that they can really call a friend. Most of the time, those that always hang out with rich people are the ones that have their own personal interest to the money or privilege just by giving that wealthy man some company.

This is not always the case, though, and does not have to be a case at all. In my observation, rich people that are taken advantage on are also those that take advantage of others. It is those people who worship their money, and think that they can buy anything and anyone because money is their super power. Well, think again if that is the case. If this is the kind of person that you are, then you are making yourself look like you are not designed to live a wealthy life. Even if you die wealthy when you are old, if you are not able to recognize what life really means and what this world really is, your existence in this world is just also going to be like a one dollar bill spent over a pack of junk food and forgotten.

It is going to be your choice whether this kind of status in life would fit you or not. Make things happen. Being rich is not always as ugly as it sounds. You can be a genuinely happy millionaire with a peace of mind. Be kind to people. Live, love, and be loved. Have a purpose and wearing a smile on your face while you walk down the streets will not be a difficult task for you.

I still believe that we are all created to be around each other. We are all stronger together. Connect with one another. If you are a wealthy man and you are in command of where the money goes, try to dedicate it in contributing value to your community. I know you would say that you earned money for yourself and not for your neighbor. Okay, fair enough. Feed yourself, get yourself clothed and sheltered. There is no single issue being able to watch over yourself; being able to prioritize what you need first. And then now, what? Will you really just keep your money in the safe? Well, okay. Maybe you want to save your fortune for the next generation. It is your choice.

But you might want to consider the fact that the best thing to really make your following generations to remember would not be how much money you left for them. Why not take a portion of what you have saved and spend it to help other really needy people? Or maybe spend that cash on a project that will contribute on making your neighborhood a safer, and a better place?

I believe that we all are given a certain power in many different forms in this life. To some, that power could have something to do with sharing their talents to the world. And for some, that power may be in a form of that millions of money that they possess. They are someone's power. That someone would have to be the one to use it, and decide where it is going to be used for. If you are a human being who recognizes that you possess a soul, a good heart, and a strong conscience, I would have to believe that you would pretty much use your power with wealth in fighting poverty.

Another thing that will determine if you are really someone who could be capable of living a wealthy lifestyle is how well you could make your own decisions. Let me repeat—your own decisions! Like I have mentioned earlier, if you are rich, you will pretty much have a lot of people surrounding you, trying to get your attention as if they would earn a dollar each time that you lay your eyes on them. Once they get you to focus on them, know that these people might have the tendency of influencing you in every single way that they would want to. They would make you believe them. They would make you do what they want you to do, and before you know it, you are already their slave when to think, yesterday you were actually paying them to do something for you.

What could happen when these people get you? They could possibly lurk you in to taking some bad vices and habits. I mean, who knows, right? It could be drugs, sex, alcohol, you name it! When you are rich, people will try to sell things to you and drain money for as long as there is something left of you up to the very last cent. I am not saying do not trust people. What I am saying is that, stay alert, and do not be stupid! Just because these people look as rich as you are does not mean they would not want your money. Be someone who deserves to handhold millions. Be smart. Watch your own steps, and be your own person of you. If you can handle all of these temptations, then by all means please stay rich and make this world a better place.

With this, I would like to take Taylor Swift as an example. Okay, I know that her family may have already been considerably well-off before she started. What I am about to tell about her is something that I just instantly remembered now as I am writing this book. Now, going back to it, Taylor is one of those many blessed people who were given the opportunity to do what she loves and got paid and rich through it. I would have to say that she had handled it very well. Maybe it also has something to do that one of her parents works in finance, but the girl managed her wealth very well—her whole career, actually. Unlike most people in Hollywood, Taylor Swift was never reported to have done drugs one single bit in her life. She

CONCLUSION

We are what we want to be. We could call ourselves however we want to be called. For me, I think we are all millionaires. We are, in fact, more than just millionaires. The only reason why people think that millions could define a person is because these people feel small. They think that money is the only thing in the world that could buy them happiness. For me the question is not whether you are a millionaire or not, but what kind of a millionaire are you?

I have said this so many times, and I will say it again—be in control of your life. No one, and no money should dictate where you are supposed to turn. May you really hold millions of dollars right now on your hand or not, it is really just all about how you add value to your existence. And we all have our in-born freedom and opportunities to make this life big, so I hope we all do aim to be a big contributor of everything that is good to this world.

The way that you are to be described is all on you. If you will be rich, it is not a sin. The only time that things really just go bad is when we give life to that money that is staring back at us. Money is not a god, and it is not a way to measure your worth because you are priceless. So be a millionaire and be happy as you live your own life and work on your own story.

About the Author

I am a millionaire. No, I do not have plenty of money in my bank account, but, I have earned more than just millions since I started working, and I am very proud to say that for those many years that I have been earning money, I earned money without even thinking how much I have already made. All I know is that I am doing what I love in something that people call a job. I am happy, I am enjoying every single minute of what I do. I love the people that surround me—they are not perfect, I know. I am not perfect, either. But I recognize that these are all part of the kind of life that I want to maintain.

The Universe has given me so much attention, that it has opened so many doors for me to share my many different talents. So, as I continue being a millionaire who live a very plain, simple, and happy life, I continue to nurture my whole being. I am very proud to see the direction that I have figured to follow, and I think that that is all that matters.

As a writer, most of you may already know how odd y style is. But it all boils down to me, wanting to keep you close to my heart and to be able to touch you in some way that I know you would remember me. Everything that I wrote in this book may or may not make much of an impression to you. But I know that somehow there would be a piece of it that you will carry with you, which would hopefully remind you of how incredible this world really is. You are bigger and more worthy than you think!

www.ingramcontent.com/pod-product-compliance
Lightning Source LLC
Chambersburg PA
CBHW030058230526
45471CB00003B/1148